Large Print

FUNNY

COLORING BOOK

For Toddlers

Ages1-3

80 pages 8,5 x 11 in

This book belongs to:

....

....

....

INTRODUCTION:

This large print funny coloring book is prepared especially for toddlers ages 1-3 so as they can enjoy these cute drawings.

This book contains 80 pages. There are enough pages for toddlers so as to get fun from this coloring activity.

We prepared large print drawings so as toddlers can learn coloring and follow the shapes easily.

As we know, kids love coloring; that's why we prepared this kind of books so as to give them this chance and let them live great moments of happiness and fun.

So, if you want that your kids get enjoyment and fun, then this is yours.

Please, for any remark about this book, this is our email : apamog@hotmail.com

THANK YOU

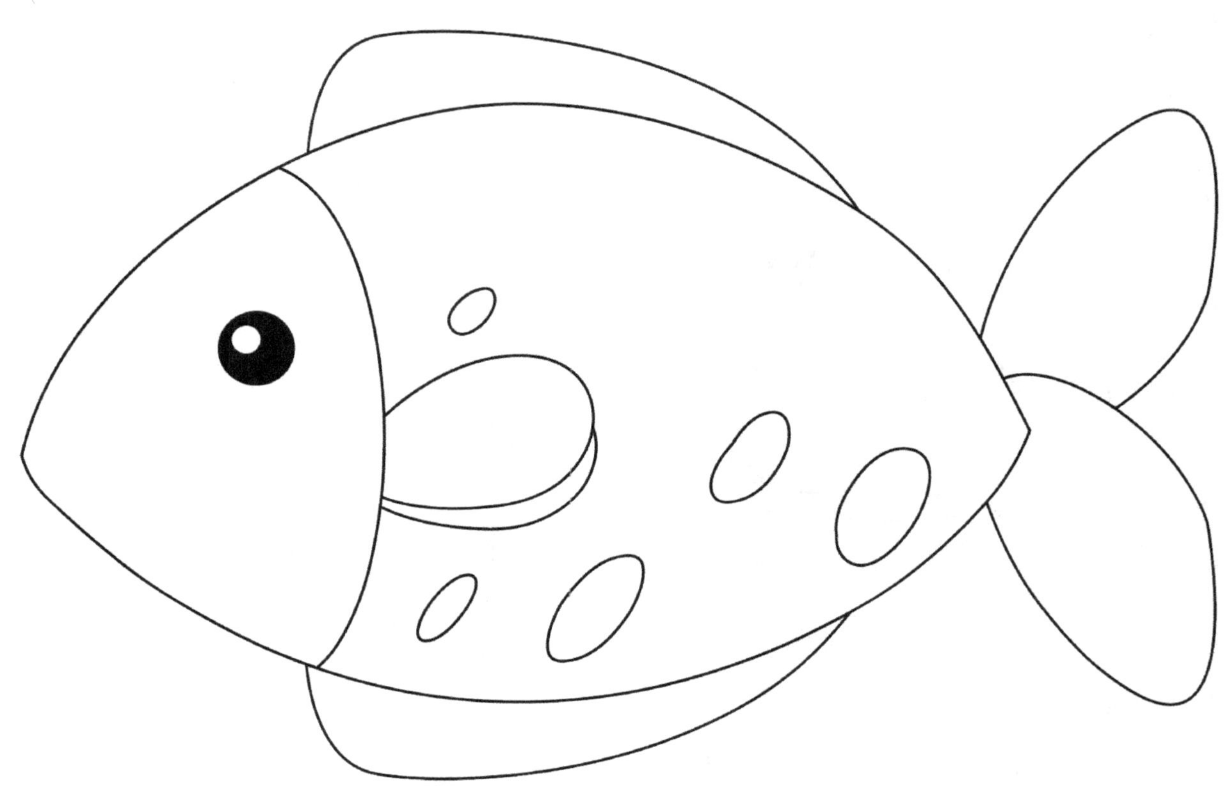

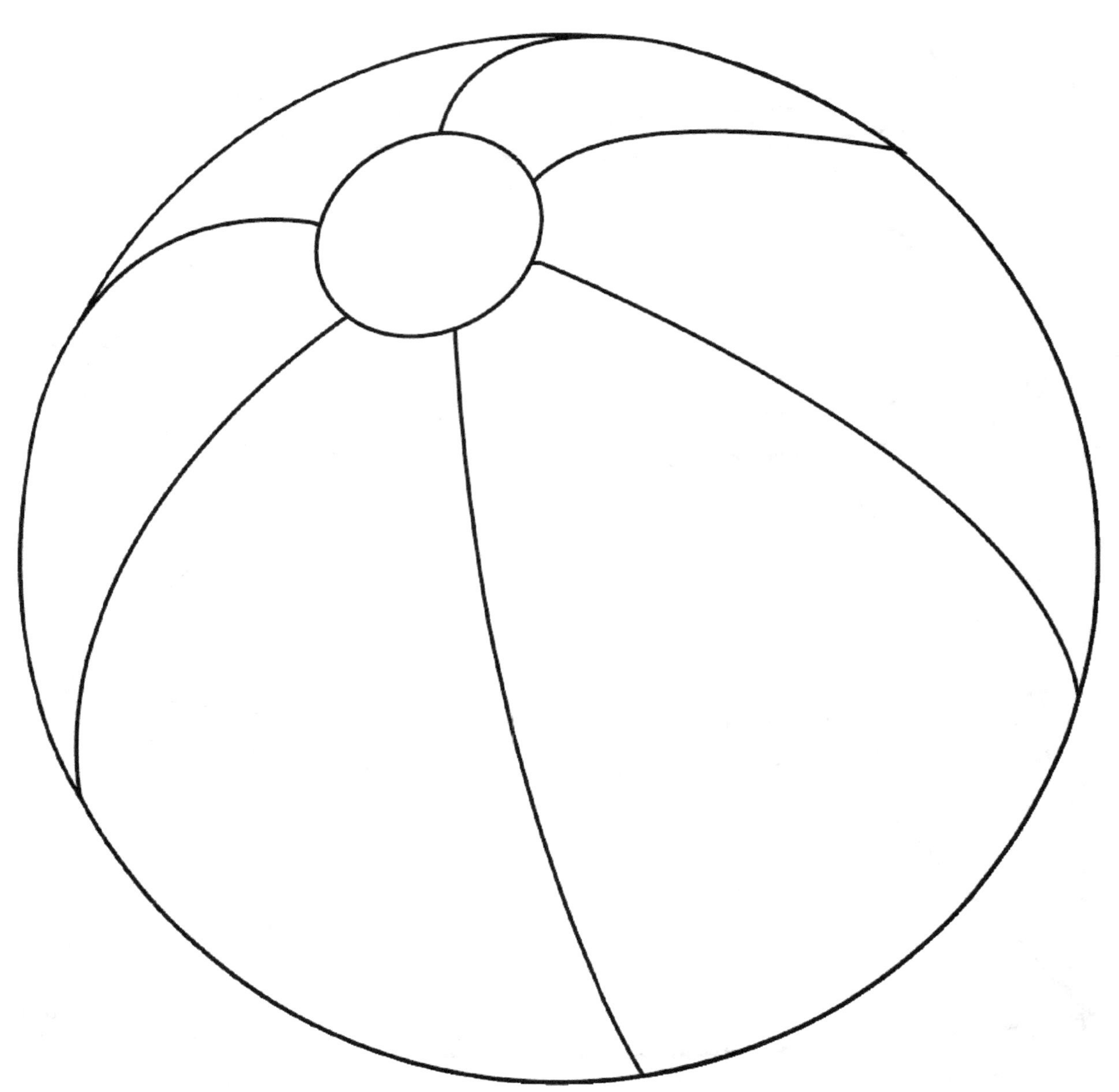

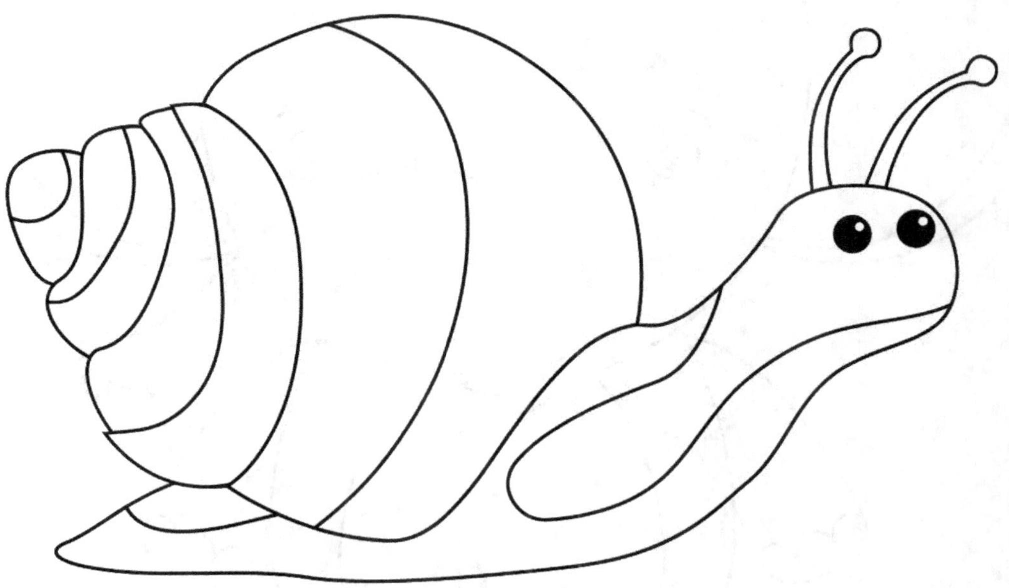

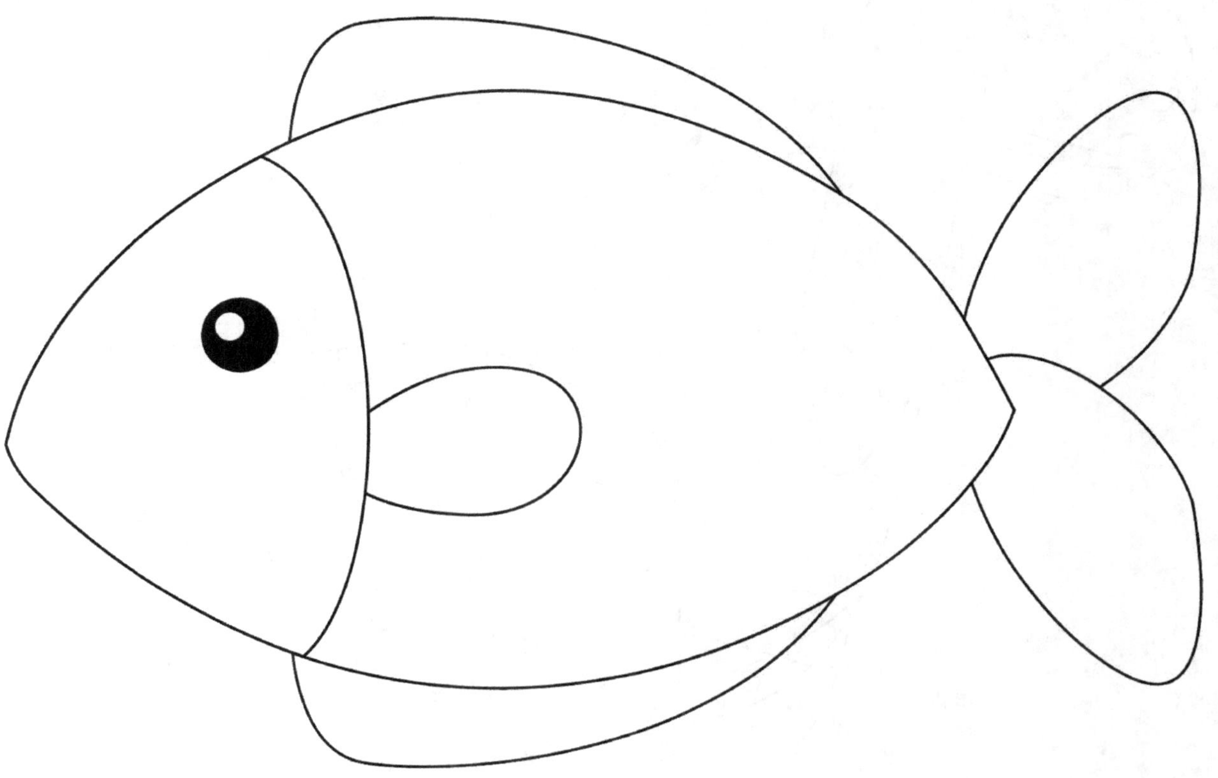

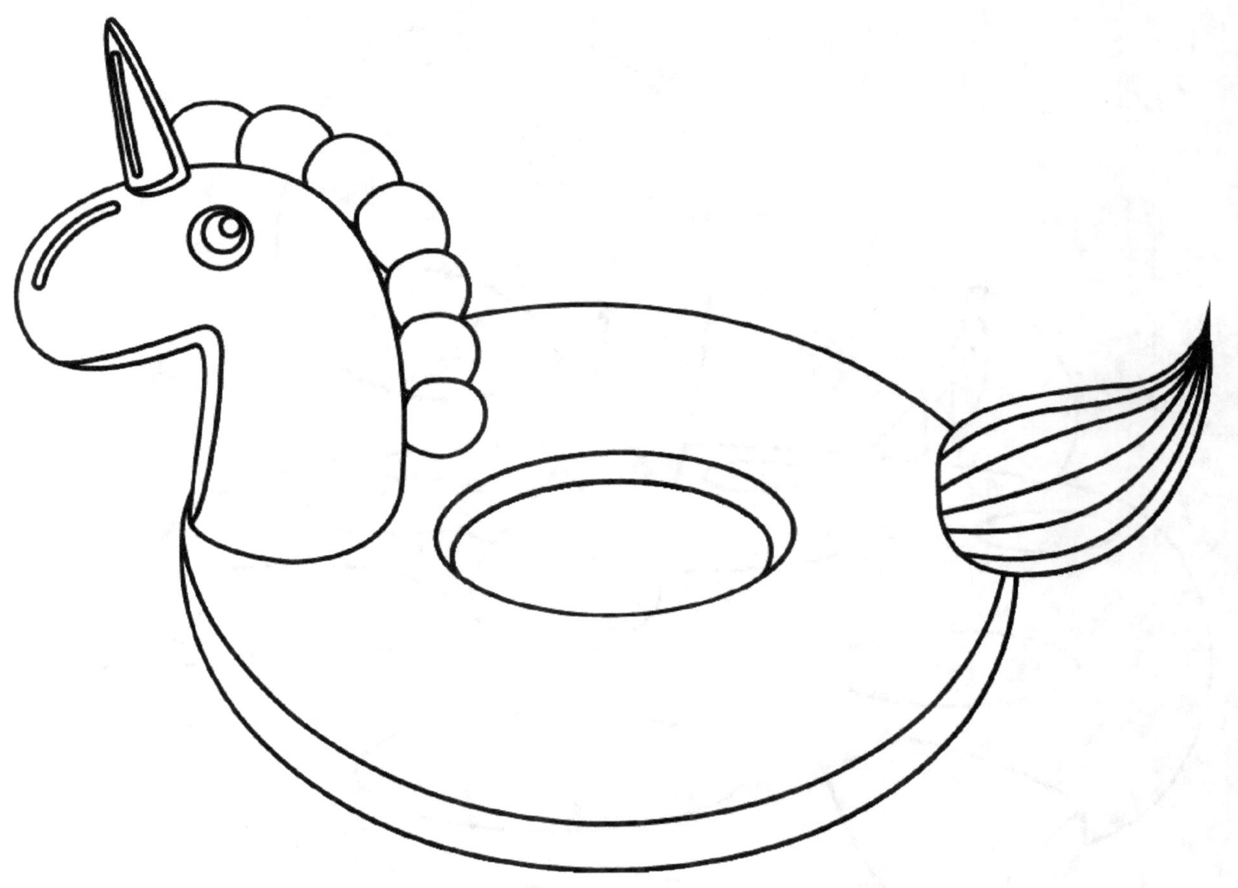

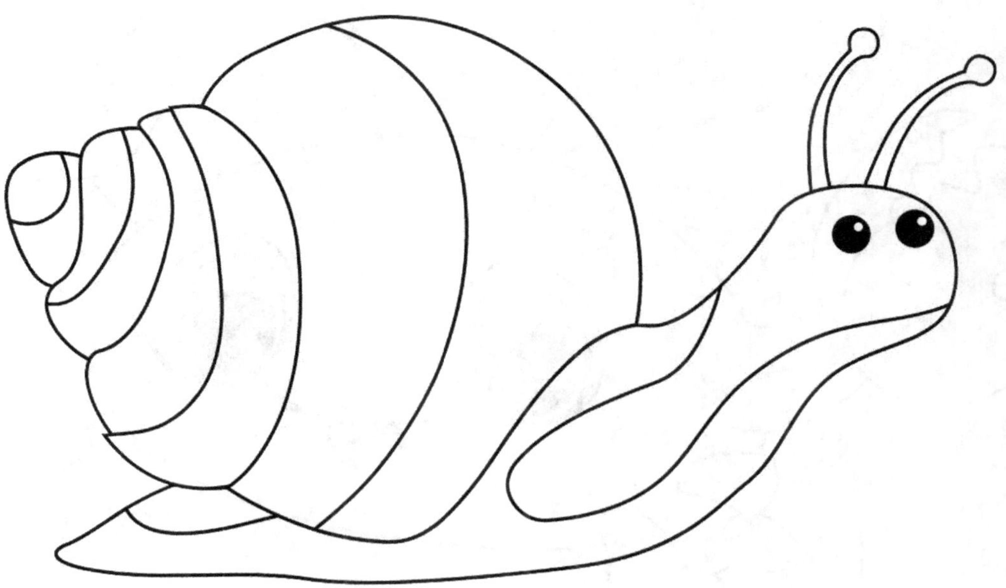

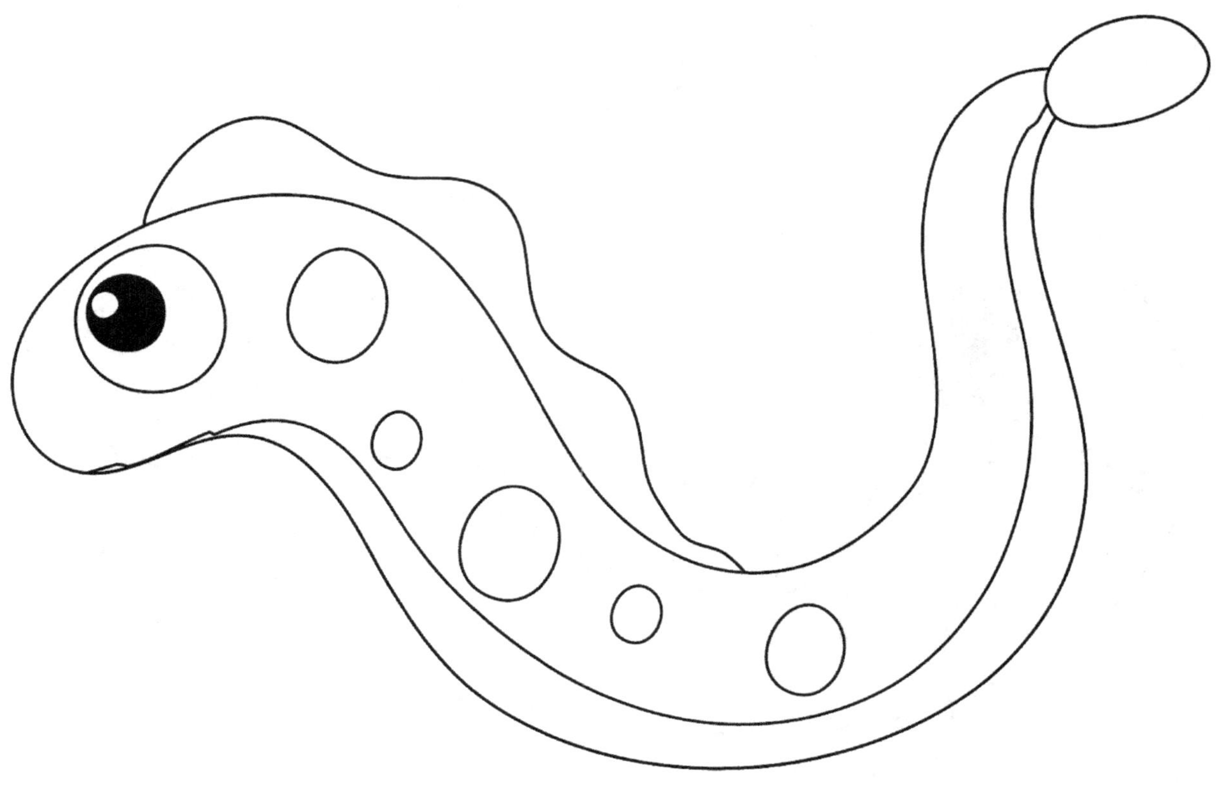